<u>football.</u>

football.

Lewis Davies

PARTHIAN

first night drama

Lewis Davies was born in Penrhiwtyn in 1967.
He has won a number of awards for his writing.

Fiction: *Work, Sex and Rugby - Tree of Crows*
My Piece of Happiness
Drama: *My Piece of Happiness - Without Leave*
Sex and Power at the Beau Rivage
Prose: *Freeways a journey West on Route 66*
As I Was A Boy Fishing

Parthian
The Old Surgery Napier Street Cardigan
SA43 1ED
www.parthianbooks.co.uk

First published in 2004 © Lewis Davies 2004
All Rights Reserved ISBN 1-902638-53-0
For performance enquiries please contact
Meg Davis, MBA, 62 Grafton Way, London
agent@mbalit.co.uk

Cover design by Marc Jennings
Printed and bound by Dinefwr Press, Llandybïe, Wales
With thanks to Steve Jon
Typeset in Caslon 540 by type@lloydrobson.com

Parthian is an independent publisher which works with
the support of the Welsh Books Council and
the Arts Council of Wales

With support from the Parthian Collective

football.

First performed at Venue 13, Edinburgh Fringe
6 August 2004

Cast:

Jason	Martin Cole
Clive	Hywel Morgan
Kate	Suzanne Procter

Director	Jeff Teare
Producer	Rebecca Gould
Assistant Director	Alex Ferris
Designer	Pete Bodenham
Sound	Dan Mitcham

In association with Made in Wales
Caribou House and Tinderbox

PARTHIAN
first night drama

Hywel Morgan is from Cardiff. He has worked in film, tv, radio and theatre all over the world including *Mill On The Floss* for Shared Experience which won the Helen Hayes Award, *Family* (LWT) and the film, *Murder by Design*. He has always wanted to add Made In Wales to the list. He now lives in London and supports Arsenal.

Martin Cole has worked as a professional actor since the age of eleven. He has worked extensively in the theatre including work at the Royal National Theatre, and played the lead role in the award winning *Starstruck* at the Tricycle Theatre, London. In the past few years he has appeared in many TV shows including *Spooks, Red Cap, Holby City* and *Family Affairs*. His film work includes *Buffalo Soldiers* with Joaquin Phoenix, and recently playing the toyboy of Rosanna Arquette in *Dead Cool*. Martin is from Cardiff, lives in London but is an international negro who drinks JD and coke (if you're asking) and supports Spurs.

Suzanne Procter was born and bred in Rochdale with the whippets. Her most recent Edinburgh experience was as Polly in the *Jolly Folly of Polly The Scottish Trolley Dolly* which went on to tour internationally. She has also appeared in *The Taming of the Shrew Interactive* at Theatre Royal Plymouth and *Pink for a Boy* at the Oldham Coliseum. She has worked in a range of tv and film productions from *Eastenders* to the *Inspector Lynley Mysteries*. She lives in Brighton and supports her husband.

football.

With thanks to Dave Roxburgh
Royal Welsh College of Music & Drama
and all at Venue 13
James Tyson
and all at Chapter
and to Othniel Smith

It's 2006. England have won the world cup. (Thank f*** – otherwise we'd have to invade Iraq again.) Sir David Beckham is a national hero. His shirt has sold for 137,000 euros at a charity auction. Three friends meet for dinner, two want sex, the other bought the shirt. It is almost ART.

A flat. London. The flat suggests money, minimalism and a taste for urban living. JASON enters. He is in his mid-thirties and slightly overweight. The man looks at a space which is the centre piece of the room. He measures it up, looks at the space. A large coat hanger floats in the space. It is supported by steel wire and weighted by a simple pulley system which connects to the ceiling by a hook and the floor by a white cube made of cement. The cement box is hollow. It has the effect of an art exhibit. It has the words White Cube Too *in black sans serif font printed on the side. A white designer chair is the only other furniture in the room.*

The buzzer rings. JASON moves across to the hallway. He exits. CLIVE enters, he puts a battered briefcase on the floor. JASON follows him into the space.

CLIVE: Where is it then?

JASON: What?

CLIVE: C'mon we've heard about it. It's in the papers.

JASON: Already?

CLIVE: Front page.

JASON: Really? You can't do anything in this city without the world knowing.

CLIVE: No, you can't do anything. I want to see it.

JASON: I haven't decided where to put it yet.

CLIVE: What's that then? *(Indicates hanger.)*

JASON: It's a suggestion.

CLIVE: More of a statement.

JASON: You're observant today.

CLIVE: It's my job.

JASON: You have a new job every month.

CLIVE: I've been at this for six months.

JASON: Liar.

CLIVE: Any wine?

JASON: I was going to ask if you would like a glass of wine, Clive.

CLIVE: Is the pope a catholic?

JASON: That's such a cliché.

CLIVE: I write for a living, what do you expect?

JASON: It's in the fridge. Bring some glasses.

CLIVE exits to the kitchen. He returns with a bottle of wine and glasses. He pours himself a glass of wine using the White Cube Too as a table. He moves to sit on the white chair.

JASON: Don't sit on the chair.

CLIVE doesn't sit on the chair.

CLIVE: You should buy red some time.

JASON: Really, any particular vintage you'd recommend?

CLIVE: No, just red.

JASON: I'd spend a fortune on new carpets.

CLIVE: I don't spill it anymore.

JASON: It's not a question of spillage. It's when you piss on the floor.

CLIVE: C'mon that was the old days. I'm reformed. I had a few demons I was trying to work out.

JASON: Anyone in particular?

CLIVE: Give me a break mun, Jase. *(He tastes the wine, finishes it, then pours himself another.)* Not too bad this. Should I like it?

JASON: Burgundy.

CLIVE: I thought burgundy was supposed to be red?

JASON: It's bleached.

CLIVE: Really. *(Reads the label on the bottle.)* Personally selected by Jason Dowe from the worlds best growers.

JASON: I didn't write the text.

CLIVE: I've seen the advert.

JASON: It's a new range, the best fifty world wines.

CLIVE: You could have taken me with you.

JASON: I didn't get to fly around the world drinking wine.

CLIVE: You mean that wasn't you on that aeroplane?

JASON: Yes it was me. It just wasn't a real aeroplane.

CLIVE: Just like this cheap fucking burgundy.

Beat. A moment of unease.

JASON: Kate is coming over *(checks his watch)* – soon.

CLIVE: Good. I haven't seen her for – must be a few months.

JASON: She mentioned it.

CLIVE: Did she?

JASON: That she hadn't seen you. Thinks you've been avoiding her.

CLIVE: Not her, just can't stand her new boyfriend. Keeps telling me how *fantastique* the French are. Merde – that's what I say to him.

JASON: I bet he's impressed with your language ability.

CLIVE: He could see I had class.

JASON: Anyway no more Michel. He's gone home.

CLIVE: Why?

JASON: I don't know.

CLIVE: You can tell me.

JASON: No I can't. She can tell you.

CLIVE: Great.

JASON: She said she'd like to see you.

CLIVE: Are you a dating agency?

JASON: Just a thought.

CLIVE: Yeah, just show me the shirt first.

JASON: I thought we would have an unveiling.

CLIVE: You wanker.

JASON: Oh c'mon, just a bit of fun. Kate will enjoy it.

CLIVE: What is she doing anyway?

JASON: You know what she is doing.

CLIVE: I see her face in the papers. I don't know what she is doing.

JASON: She's the sports editor.

CLIVE: Fuck off.

JASON: Ever since we won the world cup.

CLIVE: She's crap at sport.

JASON: She's writing about it not doing it.

CLIVE: My contention is that to write about it you've got to be able to do it.

JASON: Is that the premise of your book?

CLIVE: Fuck you.

JASON: Well done Clive, words have failed you again.

CLIVE: I'm still trying to find the through...ball.

JASON: I'm sure Kate can now discuss formations with the best of them.

CLIVE: And I can't?

JASON: I remember your 3-5-1 sweeper theory.

CLIVE: 3-5-2 with a sweeper.

JASON: Whatever. It doesn't matter.

CLIVE: It does. 3-5-1 wouldn't work.

JASON: I don't suppose it would.

CLIVE: No.

JASON: And where are you now? This new job?

CLIVE: Writing copy for *The Long View*.

JASON: *The Long View?*

CLIVE: It's a company magazine.

JASON: Anyone I've heard of?

CLIVE: Probably.

JASON: And what does *The Long View* do?

CLIVE: Make forecasts, company prospects. It's just a job while I finish the book.

JASON: The football book?

CLIVE: Yes, what else?

JASON: You've been working on it for years. Bobby Robson was captain of England when you started.

CLIVE: Bryan.

JASON: What?

CLIVE: Bryan Robson was captain. Bobby was the manager. He was the one with the Christmas tree formation.

JASON: Ever heard of hitting the Zeitgeist?

CLIVE: It's more reflective.

JASON: Perhaps Kate can help you?

CLIVE: How would she do that?

JASON: She meets the players. I read her interview with that new French guy. It was really enlightening.

CLIVE: In what way?

JASON: We got a real insight into his life. His flat in

Chelsea, his partnership in a nightclub in Paris. It was really fascinating.

CLIVE: Anything about football?

JASON: It was a human interest piece.

CLIVE: You said she was the sports editor.

JASON: Sport is now part of the culture.

CLIVE: It always was. *(The buzzer rings.)*

JASON crosses to the hallway, exits. CLIVE waits. He quickly takes another drink. JASON and KATE enter together. KATE is a modern city woman. She is looks successful and attractive.CLIVE and KATE look at each other. There is no greeting.

JASON: I'll get you a glass.

JASON leaves. KATE waits for CLIVE to speak. He doesn't.

KATE: Been a few months.

CLIVE: Has it?

KATE: Don't you remember?

CLIVE: What?

KATE: You certainly made an impression.

CLIVE: Did I?

KATE: A boys' night in. Just what I needed.

CLIVE: I don't get to stay in much.

KATE: Why should you?

CLIVE: No reason.

KATE: An aversion to your own company?

JASON: Excellent to see you both off to a good start again.

KATE: So Jason – you've got to show me. We're running it on the front page tomorrow.

CLIVE: Is that an editorial decision?

KATE: It's the cricket season or haven't you noticed?

CLIVE: I don't like cricket.

KATE: You don't like anything you don't understand.

Beat.

JASON: It's just like I remember.

Beat.

KATE: Jason, I must say I was surprised. It was so unlike you. It was so generous.

JASON: I thought it was an opportunity to put something back.

CLIVE: You needed the publicity.

KATE: Which I am sure he is about to receive. But it was still generous.

JASON: It seemed such a good cause – street children, feeding them. I couldn't resist.

CLIVE: Will that supermarket be sponsoring the soup?

KATE: Ignore him.

JASON: I've been trying for fifteen years.

KATE: Perhaps you shouldn't invite him for dinner so often?

CLIVE: The children need feeding.

KATE: And it was so much money.

CLIVE: It was a tax dodge.

KATE: Don't be so vulgar.

CLIVE: Are you telling your best friend that you won't offset it against tax?

KATE: That is not the point Clive. Other people were asked to give and they wouldn't but Jason did. By giving so generously he persuaded the others to contribute.

CLIVE: Excuse me but I believe Jason didn't give anyone anything. He paid for goods. I haven't asked how much.

JASON: It doesn't matter.

KATE: I know.

CLIVE: How?

KATE: His publicist rang to tell me.

CLIVE: Go on then.

JASON: Really this is so vulgar.

KATE: One hundred and thirty-seven thousand.

CLIVE: Fucking hell. One hundred and thirty-seven thousand euros. For a football shirt?

KATE: Yes, but it's not just any football jersey is it.

CLIVE: It's a shirt.

KATE: What?

CLIVE: It's not a jersey, it's a shirt – there's a difference.

KATE: It is a shirt that is now part of history.

CLIVE: You'll be able to put it in your memoirs. My menu of great sporting moments. The unveiling at the flat of Jason Dowe. Not exactly world history we're talking here.

KATE: Why don't you shut up.

CLIVE: Is that a put down?

JASON: He's getting at you Kate.

KATE: He always fucking gets to me. I don't know why I agreed to come.

CLIVE: You had nowhere else to go now Michel has returned to his vegetarian macrobiotic pad in Paris. What was he like as a fuck? Did he promise not to eat any of it when he went down on you?

KATE moves towards him and slaps him.

JASON: Clive, you're a pig – you always take things too far.

CLIVE: It's nothing she hasn't heard before.

KATE: Jason, I'm sorry. He provokes me. To see if I'll lose control and every time I do.

KATE leaves as JASON begins to speak.

JASON *(to crowd)*: This evening isn't going well is it? I ask two old friends over for dinner and they want to tear each other's eyes out. Do you think there's a time to leave old friendships go? Those people that you knew at university all those ten, fifteen, twenty years ago that you still feel obliged to meet once in a while. Or have you moved on? New people. I suppose I've come to the idea that Clive is a friend, a friend I've had for so long he seems part of my life. I feel sorry for him. Things never quite worked out for him. Crap career, low wages, where's under thirty thousand going to get you in London when you're thirty-five? The police earn more than that. We've all made our bit of cash but not Clive. I'll try again. Take the stuff about the price as heard. All the rest, wait and see.

The buzzer rings. JASON walks over to the hallway. Exits He returns with KATE. She kisses JASON, hands a bottle of red wine to CLIVE.

KATE: For you.

CLIVE: Thank you.

KATE: Thought you might need it.

CLIVE: Why should I?

14

KATE: It used to be your favourite drink.

CLIVE: It still is.

JASON: Excellent to see you both off to a good start again.

KATE: Yes, he always brings the best out of me.

JASON: I'm so pleased you could come.

KATE: How could I miss a dinner from the most talked about chef in London?

CLIVE: Not the best then?

KATE: I'm sure there are a few who would claim he is.

CLIVE: Apart from his publicist?

JASON: Ignore him Kate.

KATE: He's very persistent.

JASON: I was thinking of an Italian dish tonight. In celebration.

CLIVE: C'mon Jason let's see it then.

JASON: I'll get it for you. It's quite a simple hanging. Nothing too elaborate, but hell I might as well display it.

KATE: Of course.

JASON leaves. KATE looks at CLIVE.

CLIVE: What happened to Marco?

KATE: Didn't work out.

CLIVE: Why?

KATE: None of your fucking business.

CLIVE: Just asking.

KATE: So you could gloat?

CLIVE: Hell give me a break. I'm concerned about you.

KATE: Really.

CLIVE: What do you think of this shirt bollocks then?

KATE: Part of the hype.

CLIVE: But why Jason?

KATE: He likes to keep his image in the papers.

CLIVE: He's always in the fucking papers.

KATE: His last restaurant was a disaster. I wouldn't take my cat to eat there.

CLIVE: What has buying football shirts got to do with restaurant failures?

KATE: The publicity will give his new tv series a boost in ratings.

CLIVE: But he's spent a fucking fortune on this shirt.

KATE: His production company has spent the money. It's not the same thing.

CLIVE: I wish I was living in his world.

KATE: It's his last chance on the telly. If he fucks this one up they'll be looking for someone else to stir the rice.

JASON returns carrying a brown gallery purchase bag. He takes an English football shirt from it. He hangs it on the hook. Number 7, David Beckham. They look at it.

KATE: It's the real thing?

JASON: Of course it is.

KATE: Really?

JASON: Yes.

KATE: From the final?

JASON: Er no, the quarter final against Turkey.

CLIVE: It's not the one he scored the winner in then?

JASON: He's donated that to the National Gallery. The British Museum have asked for the warm up track suit.

CLIVE: What about the semi?

JASON: I'm not sure about the semi?

CLIVE: He didn't play in the fucking semi.

JASON: That's why it's not available then.

CLIVE: Are you sure this is the quarter final shirt?

JASON: There's a stain from the tackle he made just before half-time. There, look.

CLIVE takes a closer look at the shirt. JASON is nervous.

JASON: They told me all the details at the event.

CLIVE: I bet they did.

JASON: It was in the catalogue.

CLIVE: So you've paid hundred and thirty grand for a football shirt with a grass stain on it?

KATE: I think you're missing the point.

CLIVE: I wouldn't say that.

JASON: Ignore him Kate, he's trying to provoke an argument.

CLIVE: All I'm saying is that you've paid an awful lot of money for a football shirt.

JASON: I donated money to a charity. They donated me a football shirt. Is that too much for you?

CLIVE: Why the donation?

JASON: Tax.

CLIVE: So you're avoiding tax.

JASON: I'm donating to charity and buying one of the great cultural icons of our time.

CLIVE: It's not David Beckham who is hanging up there, it's his fucking shirt.

KATE: It's more than a shirt.

CLIVE: Yeh – what is it then?

KATE: It's a symbol of our times. We've won the world cup.

CLIVE: Did you put that in the Arts section?

KATE: I'm the sports editor.

CLIVE: Since when?

KATE: Don't you read the newspapers?

CLIVE: Not if I can help it.

KATE: I think Jason has been very generous.

CLIVE: Hundred and thirty grand. How much are you making on those fucking cookery books anyway?

JASON: A few bob.

CLIVE: You couldn't even do cheese on toast when I was living with you and now you're telling the educated morons of this country how to steam the perfect couscous. The society of perfect eating.

JASON: It's a process of growth.

CLIVE: And where did that London accent come from, you were a fucking Scouser ten years ago?

JASON: I've developed that's all. What have you done?

CLIVE: I've tried to be consistent.

JASON: Not original?

CLIVE: Nothing is original.

JASON: This shirt is original.

CLIVE: It's an England shirt.

JASON: Sir David Beckham's England shirt. And Clive. England is the word.

CLIVE: What's that supposed to mean?

JASON: I'm just interested in why you support England?

CLIVE: I like to move beyond national stereotypes. I see myself as an internationalist... I've got to support someone and Wales never get anywhere fucking near it.

JASON: For the final the Scottish fans were wearing Italian shirts?

CLIVE: I'm covering that in my book. It's in a chapter called Great Expectations.

KATE: What happened to your book?

CLIVE: I'm still working on it.

KATE: You've been writing it for fifteen years.

CLIVE: It's taken longer than expected. There have been a

few problems.

KATE: Remind me of the title again.

CLIVE: I've changed it.

KATE: From *How England Winning the World Cup Will Change the World*.

CLIVE: It's called *Beckham's Gold*.

KATE: Does zeitgeist mean anything to you?

CLIVE *(to the crowd)*: What is it with that word tonight? Okay so I took my time over the book. It's a big book. A moment defining book. Except the moment keeps changing. Did you ever wish the world would slow down a bit? I don't want to get off I just want a little more time in my life. Fifteen years ago I was twenty-one. I had a future. I've become my future. I drink too much. All my girlfriends hate me. My one friend is a cook with a celebrity habit. He thinks he's part of the élite because six million morons watch his tv show. Those friends on his show, they aren't his fucking friends they're actors. He hasn't got any fucking friends. Well. *(Beat.)* And Kate, what am I going to do with her? She's beautiful, successful, rich. What the fuck does she see in me? I've blown more chances than Andy Cole. What happens to your mind when you want to be with someone? That moment when you think it's all going happen between you but it never does. *Beat*. Things haven't worked out as I wanted. I can't even get seventy-five quid writing the Saturday afternoon match reports for Five Live. I wanted to be someone. I was going to be the Norman fucking Mailer of the terraces. Superman goes to the supermarket? He's gone to the supermarket but he's selling the fucking wine. Okay, I'll try again. But I still think it's fucking expensive.

JASON, KATE and CLIVE realign to look at the football shirt again.

KATE: It's almost Art.

CLIVE: Definitely.

JASON: It's just good to put something back.

KATE: It reflects the desires of the country.

CLIVE: There's even a stain on it.

JASON: Yes, when he made that tackle just before half-time.

CLIVE: In the semi?

JASON: Yes I think so.

KATE: It was a crucial moment.

CLIVE: Against the Dutch?

KATE: Saved the game for us.

JASON: I think the country has changed because of it.

CLIVE: Sure, if we hadn't won the cup perhaps we'd have had to start another fucking war? Saddam Hussein was a Manchester United supporter.

KATE: Can't say I remember his defence bringing it up.

CLIVE: They concentrated on the insanity angle. That didn't work either.

JASON: We've got a lot to thank football for.

CLIVE: It puts real life in perspective. Values.

JASON: Of course I realise there are always people willing to criticise my motives.

CLIVE: Have you had it authenticated?

JASON: What do you mean?

CLIVE: You have to get works of art verified.

JASON: Three hundred million people were watching, how much verification do you need?

CLIVE: They were watching a football game but how do you know they were watching this shirt?

KATE: It was a charity auction.

CLIVE Walks up to the shirt, feels it, then smells it.

JASON: It's been washed.

CLIVE: You've washed the sweat out?

JASON: Do you have to be so vulgar?

CLIVE: The sweat is what makes it real. The hours on the training pitch, the adrenaline rush of the game, coursing through your veins. The real game.

JASON: I'd prefer to have a clean shirt.

CLIVE: With a grass stain on it. Could have been worn on

the park by the Sunday team from the pub. Like this one. *(He takes a football shirt from his writing case.)* Same number, same colour, it's even got the grass stain. Just about in the right place. Sixty euros, Bethnall Green Road.

JASON: What are you trying to say, Clive?

CLIVE: I'm interested in your reaction. It's the same shirt. Swap you?

JASON: Fuck off.

CLIVE: C'mon you don't even know for sure who we beat in the quarter final.

JASON: I know I didn't buy it down the local Eurosport.

CLIVE: So it's not the shirt, it's the money.

JASON: It's the real fucking shirt.

CLIVE: How would you know?

JASON: It's real enough for me.

CLIVE: Of course it is.

CLIVE puts the shirt back in his case. JASON exits.

KATE: Stop it.

CLIVE: Why?

KATE: You're being horrible to him.

CLIVE: He deserves it, spending that much on a fucking

football shirt. They're sixty euros in Eurosport.

KATE: You're still being unfair. He only wanted to help.

CLIVE: Yeh, himself. What the fuck has happened to us?

KATE: We've grown up.

CLIVE: Hell no. I knew that was going to be a problem.

KATE: I did warn you.

CLIVE: And I never listened.

KATE: We all forgot that part.

CLIVE: So what happened to Miguel?

KATE: Mario went back to Turin.

CLIVE: I'm sorry to hear that.

KATE: You are not.

CLIVE: No, but I've got to appear reasonable if I want to sleep with you.

KATE: Don't bother, it doesn't suit you.

CLIVE: Didn't work out?

KATE: He kept wanting to fuck me up the arse – that good enough for you?

CLIVE: It's okay for a start.

KATE: What happened to – I'm sorry what was her name?

CLIVE: The girl at the party?

KATE: Yes, the one with the red dress.

CLIVE: I don't know.

KATE: Why not?

CLIVE: She was from an escort agency. I paid her for the night.

KATE: That's terrible.

CLIVE: Actually it was pretty good.

KATE: You must have a sad life.

CLIVE: I do. That's why I come to dinner parties at Jason's. It relieves the tedium.

KATE: So what do you really think of the jersey?

CLIVE: It's a shirt.

KATE: I know, what do you think about it?

CLIVE: He doesn't even know which fucking game it's from.

KATE: Does it matter?

CLIVE: Beckham didn't play against the Dutch. He was suspended after that linesman called him for a foul.

KATE: I think it was the referee's assistant that called the late tackle.

CLIVE: Linesman.

KATE: In the world game they are called assistants.

CLIVE: Bollocks.

KATE: You are so stubborn.

CLIVE: And?

KATE: Anyway it's part of our heritage now.

CLIVE: You would think it was important.

KATE: It's been important for the country.

CLIVE: Nonsense.

KATE: Everything is on the up, employment, property, shares. My portfolio has increased by fourteen per cent since June.

CLIVE: Mine hasn't.

KATE: Are you still poor?

CLIVE: I find money such a relative term.

KATE: You should have bought somewhere when you had a proper job.

CLIVE: I didn't want to restrict myself.

KATE: You didn't.

CLIVE: I've got used to the commuting.

KATE: Yes, where exactly are you living now? Is it on the tube?

CLIVE: I get into work.

KATE: How much did you make on the flat in Battersea?

CLIVE: That's just nasty.

KATE: Oh I'm sorry you didn't buy it did you? Property is theft remember.

CLIVE: It certainly was in my case.

KATE: And work? Where is Wales's answer to Rimbaud prostituting himself now?

CLIVE: I'm writing predictions for *The Long View*. It's a spiritual magazine.

KATE: You're an atheist.

CLIVE: A spiritual atheist.

KATE: Do you think you might have made a few mistakes in your life?

CLIVE: What am I supposed to say to that?

KATE: The truth?

CLIVE: How far will that get me?

KATE: It might help to talk to someone.

CLIVE: I don't think so.

KATE: I'll see if Jason needs some help.

KATE exits. CLIVE looks at the shirt. He lowers the shirt, slips it from the hanger. He places the replica shirt from his writing case on the hanger and winches it up.

JASON arrives back. He takes a sip of wine. He looks at the shirt.

JASON: Dinner won't be long but I've forgotten the basil. There'll be some at the Indian shop on the corner. Do you mind?

CLIVE: Of course not.

JASON: Just down the road. It's open all night.

CLIVE: Basil? What does it look like?

JASON: It has big green leaves. They reduce really easily into this sauce that...

CLIVE: C'mon.

JASON *(realising he's been had)*: A big bunch.

CLIVE: No problem.

CLIVE exits. JASON walks over and checks the shirt. He feels the fabric. KATE walks in.

KATE: Checking your investment?

JASON: Do you think I've been rather foolish?

KATE: Not at all.

JASON: It does seem rather a lot of money now.

KATE: You've bought one of the great cultural symbols of our time.

JASON: I don't even like football.

KATE: It was for a good cause.

JASON: There is that, I suppose.

KATE: And you can put it against tax.

JASON: I'll need to.

KATE: Clive was impressed.

JASON: Then he's a bigger fool than me.

KATE: Football was his life for years.

JASON: I never understood that about him. He used to watch the scores on a Saturday afternoon in the pub and get really excited if Manchester United beat Chelsea. Why?

KATE: It's a male hormone.

JASON: I haven't got it.

KATE: I don't think you have.

JASON: It's nothing to do with my sex life.

KATE: Clive just can't believe he's grown up. He's thirty-five, no kids, no wife and he's never going to make it into the third division reserves.

JASON: It's all over then.

KATE: It is for Clive.

JASON: What about the book? You must know some publishers?

KATE: The moment has gone.

JASON: I thought you said it was good?

KATE: It was – when he started it. But you've got to finish a book.

JASON: What about a sports column?

KATE: Please, we'd kill each other.

JASON: You think so?

KATE: Anyone can write for the papers. You've just got to choose who you sleep with first.

JASON: Surely you're not as cynical as Clive?

KATE: They just don't take you seriously. I know the game. I've researched it. I've written some ground breaking articles on player profile. A real insight into their lives but I might as well be writing for the women's page. In the end we all get fucked.

JASON: Mario didn't work out?

KATE: He got offered a job in Turin.

JASON: You didn't want to go with him?

KATE: Sure, he didn't want me.

JASON: I see.

KATE: He lived in my flat for six months. Didn't give me anything for the rent. I thought I was in love. I was in love.

JASON: I thought he was a lovely boy. He said lovely things about my cooking.

KATE: He wanted to fuck you as well.

JASON: I didn't mean it like that.... It just happened.

KATE: What happened?

JASON: Nothing... much. It sort of got out of context.

KATE: I didn't know there was anything to get out of context?

JASON: That weekend you were in Barcelona. He called up, suggested we have some dinner. It was all very casual. He came here. We drank some wine, as you do. He told me about his family in Turin. They sounded very nice, accommodating. Not like mine. We had things in common. It was nice to talk art, food, even football. I didn't mean anything to happen. I mean I didn't know he was, well, interested. It didn't happen again. Just the once.

KATE: Jason what are you telling me?

JASON: Nothing, nothing at all. Just an evening together.

KATE: You fucked Mario?

JASON: I'm sorry, Kate. I really am.

KATE: I can't believe it.

JASON: Nor me. It was, you know... spontaneous.

KATE: He always was.

JASON: I'm really sorry.

KATE: I can't believe I'm still so stupid. I actually trust men.

JASON: Kate, don't.

KATE: Every time I believe what they say.

JASON: We're not all the same.

KATE: Is it genetic you think? Once you start getting wet your brain gives up. He wants to fuck me. He must love me. We'll have children. Am I missing something here?

JASON: I'm really, really sorry. We all make mistakes.

KATE: You made any others lately? You fucked Clive as well?

JASON: I have my standards.

KATE: Not at that restaurant.

JASON: Signing the lease was a mistake.

KATE: The food was fucking crap.

JASON: It was supposed to be a design concept.

KATE: People wanted to be fed not fleeced.

JASON: I'll see if the sauce is simmering yet...

CLIVE walks in, senses the atmosphere. He passes JASON a bag of herbs.

CLIVE: Here's the herbs.

JASON: I said basil.

CLIVE: So?

JASON: This is oregano.

CLIVE: They're Italian. What's the difference?

JASON: I haven't time to explain.

CLIVE hands JASON the basil which he has been concealing.

CLIVE: There's something burning here?

JASON: I can't smell anything.

CLIVE: What about you Kate?

KATE: No, nothing.

CLIVE: Funny that. I'm sure someone was cooking cheese on toast.

JASON: I'll get the tomato sauce going.

JASON exits.

KATE: The best chef in London can't cook pasta properly.

CLIVE: What happened?

KATE: We had a heart to heart.

CLIVE: Dangerous.

KATE: Do you want sex tonight?

CLIVE: Were you always so charming?

KATE: I've decided you might be worth it.

CLIVE: My technique has improved.

KATE: I should hope so.

CLIVE: How would you know?

KATE: Everyone said you were crap.

CLIVE: I didn't realise you swapped notes.

KATE: Just funny stories.

CLIVE: Why wouldn't you sleep with me before?

KATE: You were always drunk.

CLIVE: I was scared you were going to say no.

KATE: I was always going to say no when you were drunk.

CLIVE: It wasn't meant to be an insult.

KATE: It was hardly a compliment.

CLIVE: I'm not drunk yet.

KATE: You're an alcoholic.

CLIVE: Just because I drink doesn't mean I'm an alcoholic.

KATE: You'll find they are the same thing eventually.

KATE takes a drink from her glass. She walks over to CLIVE and kisses him. She turns to the crowd.

KATE: I know, I don't really know what I see in him either. Apart from he's available. He used to be fun. He'd create a few stories by just being Clive. The lovable drunk. I thought I'd grow out of him. Find someone I'd connect with. My other half. But I've met so many wankers. Men who think they are still living with their mother. Men who can't communicate. They never talk to you. They never ask what I want. Why I'm doing this. Where I'm from. Mario thought Rochdale was the last stop on the Northern Line. Life didn't exist beyond London, Torino and Easy Jet. I knew he'd fucked Jason. I could see their unease, the smirk on Mario's face. His mother's welcome to him. At least Jason told me. He's clueless really – another big hairy boy – he used to call me mother when I was living with him. Funny that. I rather liked being his mother. He'd come in crying after yet another boyfriend drama and I would hold him and he'd fall asleep with me. My own little boy – still. Then Clive would come in drunk, call Jason a big scouse poof and that would be the end of a beautiful evening. It would always come back to Clive. He'd always see the shit and make us laugh about ourselves. They're all still boys. Big, hairy boys playing at being men. But now I want to play.

She turns to CLIVE.

KATE: Give me the jersey.

CLIVE: The what?

KATE: The shirt then.

CLIVE: Why?

KATE: Guess.

CLIVE: You can't do that.

KATE: Why not?

CLIVE: It's Jason's.

KATE: You said he didn't know which shirt it was anyway.

CLIVE: But he will.

KATE: He won't know the difference.

CLIVE: He's probably had it DNA tested.

KATE: It's been washed.

CLIVE: Think about this carefully Kate.

KATE: I have. Jason doesn't really want it. He hates the game. I have plans for this one.

CLIVE: Which are?

KATE: I'm going to fuck you – with it on.

CLIVE: I'm not sure I want to sleep with David Beckham.

KATE: We'll swap half way through.

CLIVE: No.

KATE: You can go on top.

CLIVE: It's... just that maybe we could do it without the shirt.

KATE: No shirt, no sex.

CLIVE *turns to see if JASON is there and then to the crowd)*: Ok. *(He passes the shirt to KATE. She swaps the shirts.)*

CLIVE: He'll notice.

KATE: No, he won't.

She stuffs the shirt in her bag. CLIVE hangs the shirt back up. He caresses it.

CLIVE: The grass stain's in the right place?

JASON walks in. CLIVE is looking closely at the shirt.

JASON: Taking a closer look?

KATE: Feeling the width, as it were.

CLIVE: Just checking for authenticity. You might need to sell it one day.

JASON: I wouldn't have thought so. I think I'll let one of the art galleries borrow it for the new season.

CLIVE: They won't hang it.

JASON: Why not?

CLIVE: Who is the artist?

JASON: Everyone is implicated.

KATE and CLIVE hold a moment of guilt.

JASON: Would you like to move to the dining room?

CLIVE and KATE exit. The lights dim. JASON looks at the shirt, then to see if his guests have left. He looks at Clive's writing case. Opens it. He takes the shirt from the case, looks at the shirt hanging up. He compares the two shirts.

Martin Cole, Suzanne Procter, Hywel Morgan

PARTHIAN new drama includes work by:

Lucinda Coxon
Gwenno Dafydd
Lewis Davies
Siân Evans
Lucy Gough
Mark Jenkins
Patrick Jones
Afshan Malik
Sharon Morgan
Alan Osborne
Ian Rowlands
Othniel Smith
Ed Thomas
Frank Vickery
Christine Watkins
Roger Williams

For a full catalogue www.parthianbooks.co.uk

"Parthian has a well-deserved reputation as the most vigorous publishing house in Wales, bringing old and new writers to their readers."
Planet

Jeff Teare, Alex Ferris